TOUGH *Girls*

MY EXPERIENCE

Laverne Richardson

JT Publishing
www.jottingtruth.com

Tough Girls

Copyright © 2017 by LaVerne Richardson

Published by JT Publishing

Charlotte, NC 28273 www.jottingtruth.com

No part of this publication may be reproduced, stored in a retrieval system, or transmitted in any form or by any means, electronic, mechanical photocopying, recording, scanning, or otherwise, except as permitted under Section 107 or 108 of the1976 United States Copyright Act, without either the prior written permission of the author or authorization through payment of the appropriate per-copy fee to the Copyright Clearance Center, Inc. 222 Rosewood Drive, Danvers, MA 01923, 978-750-8400, fax 978-646-8600, or on the Web at www.copyright.com. Requests to the author for permission should be addressed to the Permissions Department, LaVerne Richardson.

Limit of Liability / Disclaimer: The advice and strategies contained herein may not be suitable for your situation. You should consult with a professional where appropriate. Neither the publisher nor the author shall be liable for any loss of profit or any other commercial damages, including but not limited to special, incidental, consequential, or other damages.

Readers should be aware that Internet websites offered as citations and / or sources for further

information may have changed or disappeared between the time this was written and when it is read.

Scriptures taken from the Holy Bible, New International Version®, NIV®. Copyright© 1973, 1978, 1984, 2011 by Biblica, Inc.™ Used by permission of Zondervan. All rights reserved worldwide. www.zondervan.com The "NIV" and "New International Version" are trademarks registered in the United States Patent and Trademark Office by Biblica, Inc.™

Other Scripture references are from the following sources:New King James Version®. Copyright© 1982 by Thomas Nelson. Used by permission. All rights reserved.

Jotting Truth books and products are available through most bookstores. To contact Jotting Truth visit www.jottingtruth.com.

Library of Congress Cataloging-in-Publication Data

Richardson, LaVerne, 1956—

Tough girls: my experience / LaVerne Richardson.

ISBN 978-0-9909925-1-6 (paperback); ISBN 978-0-9909925-3-0 (ebk)

2017941407

Printed in the United States of America

10 9 8 7 6 5 4 3 2 1

Contents

Acknowledgements		VII
Foreword		XIII
Introduction		XV
Round 1	The Past	1
Round 2	Leah	7
Round 3	The Choice	15
Round 4	Disability	23
Round 5	The Sacrifice	33
Round 6	Twelve Years	43
Round 7	My Naomi	49
Round 8	Sarah	57
Round 9	The Final Round	65
About the Author		71

Acknowledgements

With so many to thank, I feel compelled to start with my two greatest supports, my daughter Jossalyn R. Wilson, and my god-son Marcel Anderson. I love you both so much. You two have held my hand, prayed with me, cried with me, and kicked my butt to finish. I am so grateful for your love and support. I cannot thank you enough, and I surely cannot repay you for all you have done for me during this process.

Brandon, Rashad, and Marquis, you are my three wise men. You three are smart, strong, and courageous. I am proud to call you my sons, and I am forever grateful that God chose me as your mother. You guys made me a better person; because of you I am stronger, more courageous, and adventurous. You have allowed me to meet people I never thought I would meet, go places and experience things I never thought I would experience. You and your sister gave me strength to climb without fear, and I love all of you so much.

Darryl, thank you for your love and support. You too are an asset to our family. I believe God's addition is wonderful. He always adds what you need, when you need it, and we needed you. You are loved.

Christopher Luke, you are the joy of my life. You give me so much, much more than you will ever know in your lifetime. I am so grateful God allows me to live on this earth and be your Nana. I would not trade this experience for the world. I call your mom "My Sunshine." I was very young when I had your mom, and she and your uncles brought a light to my life that I never imagined. The five of us went through some dark and rainy days; you are our little rainbow. I thank God for you, and I love you!

Mama, "Cat," you were the first person I met, and I believe it was love at first sight. You have provided me with more than you will ever know and more than I could ever voice. I love you! Thank you for not thinking of it as robbery to give me life, or share your life with me. You Mama, are my friend.

Sissy! Marquita, I love you! Thank you for believing I am great. I do not know why, but you make me want to become great just for you. Thank you for not only being my sister, but also being my friend.

Thank you to my three best friends. Yes, three! Some people do not have one best friend, but I am blessed with three, Patty, Corchanda, and Altie.

Patty, we have been together since I was three years old. We rode our bikes together, stayed up late talking about boys, ate each other's food, and drank from the water hose. We have gotten into and out of trouble (a few times ending with us grounded), and still, we are together! We never stopped loving each other, even when things separated us. We held each other dear in our hearts. When I shared with you I was writing a book, you said, "I am so proud! My sister is going to become an author." Gosh, if you only knew what your words meant to me; I am forever your sister and best friend. I love you Patty Woodruff.

Corchanda, I think we met in 1995. When we first met, I never imagined we would be as close as we are today. However, once we got to know each other, I could not imagine life without you. God knew I needed you, and I still need you today. You came into my life when I was a single mom, struggling, and you were three years younger than me, a college graduate, with no children. Yet, you moved to Spartanburg, and you helped me. You helped in ways you may not have even realized. You have been my leaning post no matter the situation, and I pray I have been that for you as well. I love ya gal, more than words could ever express!

Altie, you are more like an auntie, and YOU ROCK! The love, encouragement, conversations, and wisdom you have shared with me are priceless treasures. I love you lady!

Pastor and Co-Pastor Jenkins, thank you for your love and teachings. Because of you, I see myself in scripture and know if God be for me, nothing and no one can be against me. I love you both!

First Baptist Church of Fairforest, each of you are so dear to me. The love we share, the memories we have made collectively and one on one, have been both enriching and rewarding. I cannot thank you enough for helping me through the journey of life. I am grateful for the old, the young, and the ones who have gone before us. I would not be who I am today if it had not been for your love and support. Through all my mix-ups and mess-ups, you have always loved me and encouraged me to hold to God's unchanging hand. I am wiser, and I know how to love others because of you. Thank you; I love you!

Uncles, while I miss the three of you who are with the Lord, I am grateful to have two of you here to cherish. The five of you helped raise me. You made me TOUGH! I wish I could express what each of you mean to me. Tot, Ed, Jerry, Tommy, and Clint, I love you!

Minnie, Mattie, and Para Lee, you were the world's best grandmothers. I miss you three dearly, and I love you so much. Thank you for your love, special moments, and the ways you made me feel. While gone, you three live in my heart. You will never be forgotten.

Daddy, I miss you so much. I feel like you were gone too soon, but everything I needed to become TOUGH in this world God allowed you to give and show me. I will forever share your ways and your love with your grandkids and those around me. I love and miss you Leonard Richardson!

James and Mary Woodruff, you are the best godparents. WOW! I do not know if you realized you were teaching me! I think you were just loving God and trying to make me and Patty "do right." You two gave me more than you will ever know, I love you.

Special love and appreciation to Josephine Hughes, Flossie Hughes, Mary Dease, Pamela Mitchell, Josephine Geter, Dorothy Black, Mary Smith, JoAnne Miller, Donald and Dollie Gibson, Willa Reeder, Deacon Walker Lee, and Clarence "June Bug" and Catherine Taylor.

Darnell, I could not leave you out. Thank you for making these past few months amazing. Sharing your love and your laughter has made my world a better place, and I look forward to whatever plan God has for us.

For 20 years, I have worked for my agency; each of you in that world are awesome! Thank you.

Family members, and friends I have adopted as family along the way, I love and thank you for your support.

Finally, to my enemies, I love and thank you too.

Foreword

Something profound happens internally and externally when we make meaning of our experiences. Our choices, adversities, and victories have a different weight.

LaVerne has beautifully made meaning of her experiences, captured the essence of how God's word, His women, and their stories, align to situations faced by women today.

Using the most intimate parts of her journey, she freely shares her story and how God revealed Himself and His love to her throughout scripture.

This book contains wisdom that will help you think critically and spiritually about experiences you encounter. It will encourage you, ensuring that you have not, will not, and do not struggle alone.

It will remind you that every hardship, mountain, or seemingly impossible hike is worth the tattered clothing, bruised knees, and bloody knuckles.

Tough girls do not back down, they do not stop fighting, and they do not give up because they know pressing produces the prize, who is Christ Jesus.

I am fortunate that I not only get to read Laverne's lessons, but as her daughter, I am a part of her story. Watching her live her truth and now share her victory, has been, and remains my greatest influence.

Her work reminds women that fighting is a part of the journey, however, we are strong enough, smart enough, and TOUGH enough to overcome with God on our side.

Make no mistake, those who suffer with Him will reign with Him.

Lean into LaVerne's teachings and embrace her tough moments; you will indeed find meaning, make meaning, and realize you too are a Tough Girl!

Jossalyn Richardson Wilson
Proud Daughter
Founder, Jossalyn's Journey

Introduction

Throughout my life, I have faced challenges and situations that attempted to leave me empty, discouraged, and counted out.

However, those seemingly diminishing and damaging events did not break me.

I used my experiences to learn what God's word says about me, about my struggles, and about my hardships. As a result, I chose to believe His word as the truth about my life and my story, and I chose to accept victory as my outcome.

My prayer for you as you read *Tough Girls*, is that you think about your life's experiences. Think about the journeys you have traveled, what you have learned, and more importantly, what God says about your path.

There is a Ropes Course at the end of each round (chapter). Engage by answering the questions, think about the impact your responses have on you, and how it shows up in your life and relationships.

Remember, every day is not easy, and every moment is not certain, but our God is faithful and His promises are "yes and Amen" (2 Corinthians 1:20).

You are tough! Embrace it, celebrate it, and let the world know you are a winner!

ROUND 1
The Past

When I think of women in the Bible, the word tough comes to mind. Rahab decided to hide the spies so she and her family could experience freedom; she was a tough girl.

The woman who decided to give up her child so that he would not be subjected to the brutal death of being cut in half, she was a tough girl.

Ruth, gave up the familiar for the unfamiliar, another tough girl.

There was Sarah, who assumed she made a wise decision when she encouraged her husband to conceive a child with their handmaid, Hagar. However, after offering the knowledge of adultery to her husband, she delivered her own child. She was a tough girl.

Leah, loved a man who did not love her.

Eve was forced to accept her child was a murderer.

Rebekah faced the reality that she turned her child into a deceiver.

Eunice and Lois taught their son and grandson to display moral qualities despite his father's wrongdoing.

The woman who lived with the stigma of five husbands who did not belong to her, the woman who bled for twelve years, afraid she would never be well, the two sisters who watched their brother die while they waited for their good friend Jesus to come, and Mary, who witnessed her son suffer on a cross and die for all of mankind—those women were tough girls.

These women experienced tough times, making decisions for the moment they were facing.

Truthfully, we all face things.

However, have you considered that our trials are momentary?

1 Peter 5:10 states, "After you have suffered a little while, the God of all grace, who has called you to his eternal glory in Christ, will himself restore, confirm, strengthen and establish you."

This scripture implies that our suffering has meaning, and it produces God's promise of restoration, confirmation, strength, and establishment.

Sometimes it is difficult to believe we will be restored, confirmed, strengthened, and established by God because as women we often endure and face so much.

It can sometimes feel we must remain strong and tough against all odds.

I often think women are God's toughest creation. I am sure some men may not agree with me, but think about it.

Women carry and birth children—that alone makes us tough. There are also women who have carried children and faced loss; I believe that experience makes one tougher.

There are women who have faced sickness, heartbreak, grief, disappointment, and betrayal, and throughout each moment they were faced with a decision—a tough decision.

Face it, women are tough by design!

There are choices we have made that do not make us proud. There are decisions that did not end as we thought or planned. Yet we decided, and here we are today—more resilient, wiser, and tougher.

Sometimes the moments we experience feel so overwhelming we want to abandon life or the situation because it feels and appears easier to throw up our hands and walk away. However, in those moments we experience growth, and we learn the magnitude of our strength.

I have been hurt and even betrayed throughout my life, and I have faced situations and experiences that have left me wondering how I made it out or through that time with victory!

However, I have learned as believers, our suffering places a mandate on God's victory.

What an amazing God, one who allows something painful to harvest His precious victory.

Yes, we may experience weeping night after night, face demons at work day after day, or at church Sunday after Sunday.

However, God miraculously brings us out of every situation better than before, and better than we imagined.

He did the same for women in scripture, and He continues to deliver and bring us out today.

How do you see yourself?

Do you see yourself breaking free from the bondage that attempts to keep you?

I learned how I viewed the situation, and how I viewed myself throughout my circumstances impacted the outcome.
How I carried myself, not just acting like a lady, but thinking

and believing I was strong, helped chart my course. I knew in some ways I messed up, and I knew I made the wrong choices. However, what I believed about myself, and the story I chose to accept as truth (God's word), helped me continue each round of the fight.

Sometimes we will wrestle with the enemy, but we must believe we have what it takes to knock that joker down. Remember, just like our biblical sisters, we have what it takes to trust God no matter what.

We are tough girls!

Ropes Course

Take an opportunity to reflect and respond to the questions and statements below.

Does your past keep you from moving forward with God and His plan for your life?

Do you struggle to trust God based on your circumstances?

ROUND 2
Leah

Leah was Rachel's older sister, and she was often noted as unattractive.

Although deemed unattractive, according to their customs, she was expected to get married first, as it was a disgrace for the younger daughter to wed before the eldest daughter.

However, Jacob, Esau's twin, and noted deceiver, fell in love with Rachel. He asked his uncle Laban, their father, for her hand in marriage.

Their father agreed to Jacob's request. However, he tricked Jacob and gave him Leah instead, as he wanted to ensure his eldest daughter wed first.

When Jacob found out he had been deceived, he was upset. However, he was so in love with Rachel he agreed to stay married to Leah and work for their father for many more years in hopes of having her.

Meanwhile, Leah had six sons and one daughter with Jacob; she was a faithful wife and worked hard alongside him.

Her efforts, however, did not seem to matter to Jacob. He wanted Rachel.

Have you ever been in that type of situation, one in which you were made to feel you were not pretty or attractive?

Have you ever felt like your beauty was not the "right" beauty?

I am certain Leah struggled with those feelings and thoughts, and I believe many of us wrestle with those same emotions today because we have accepted someone else's perception of us.

Know, your beauty is hidden deep in the heart, hidden in your very being.

Your beauty cannot be seen when someone approaches you because your beauty is concealed in the crevices of your soul, and it is only revealed when an individual truly gets to know you.

I will be the first to admit, I believed this type of hidden beauty was the wrong type of beauty.

Like Leah, I have felt the pain of not being considered one of the pretty girls.

I thought I was beautiful, but it did not seem like anyone else truly saw my beauty.

There were days I came home from school and cried.

There were days I tried to look a certain way, or act a certain way because I believed beauty was outward, and I thought I needed to live up to a certain standard of beauty.

You know, the beauty that suggests if you look the part, have the right hairstyle, the right makeup, and the right clothes, you are beautiful. I even believed hanging out with popular people made beautiful.

Unfortunately, I did not realize those things did not make me beautiful.

My attempts, instead, caused me to keep getting into messes to look a part that I did not understand.

Leah was given to Jacob. I, however, gave my love, devotion, and bared a child with a man who did not see my beauty. He used me for what he needed or wanted at the time, but never really saw me. There were nights I stayed awake trying to understand, and trying to figure it out. When I acknowledged the truth of the situation, it was painful.

When I recognized my beauty, and started to fight from a place of determination, God gave me victory.

My beauty did not emerge until I realized the beauty I possessed, I was hiding.

My beauty was not hidden, I was hiding it.

I did not need anyone to see it. I had to see it.

We are beautiful when we see our beauty.

You are the only one who knows the real you, and when you accept the real you and stop trying to get people to see your beauty through outward adornment, you become beautiful.

In that moment, you begin to fight from a place of victory.

Rather than trying to overcome defeat, you know you are a winner.

True beauty is loving your neighbor as yourself. True beauty is acknowledging your sister is hurt, and instead of whispering about her situation you call her to pray, and you ask God to help even if you are in a situation yourself.

True beauty is meeting a man who is married and letting him know you are your sister's keeper.

It is being true to yourself when you know you deserve more or better than what someone is giving you.

True beauty is not holding bitterness and malice in your heart because someone hurt you.

True beauty cannot be seen in your physical appearance; rather, it is glimpsed when someone really knows and understands you.

There is beauty in carrying the spirit of God, as His spirit outshines any designer bag, clothing, or makeup.

Having His beauty opens us up for the opportunity to be loved.

His beauty allows us to sow seeds of love and kindness, which in turn brings love back to us—true love, the love we read about in scripture. God's love is not self-seeking or boastful. It is not rude, and it does not envy others.

Only God can send that type of love, as He is the only one who can teach us how to love ourselves and others. When we have His love resonating in and through our being, it can be felt by all.

That beauty, is God's glory.

Leah's pain could have become detrimental, but like so many of us, her pain became her victory.

Allow your pain to become your victory.

Get in the fight, but enter with victory in your heart.

No matter the labels placed on you by the world, no matter who walks away, who does not see your beauty, or who does not acknowledge your value, know your worth. Beauty is more than your outward appearance; it is also what you possess inside.

This type of love, this type of beauty, helps you win the round.

Ropes Course

Take an opportunity to reflect and respond to the questions and statements below.

Would you use the word beautiful to describe yourself?

If not, what is keeping you from seeing yourself as beautiful?

Is so, what characteristics make you beautiful?

Do you see yourself as victorious?

Describe what makes you victorious.

ROUND 3
The Choice

1 Kings 3:16-28 recounts the story of two women who lived in the same house. Both women delivered their sons around the same time.

One night, while sleeping, one mother rolled on her baby, and he died.

While the other mother slept beside her son, the mother of the dead child switched the boys.

The next morning, when the mother got up to feed her baby, she saw he was dead. After looking at the child further she realized it was not her son. The women took the matter to King Solomon to share the dilemma.

The woman of the dead son argued that the other woman was wrong and suggested her son was dead.

The women continued to argue about the matter in front of King Solomon.

To decide who was being truthful, King Solomon asked for a sword. He decided to cut the child in half, giving each woman part of the child.

When King Solomon announced his decision, the real mother spoke up and asked him not to cut the child in half. She professed that she would rather have the other woman take him, if it meant her son could live. Meanwhile, the other woman voted to kill the child.

Based on the real mother's plea, the king did not kill the baby boy, and he returned him to his natural mother.

A true parent willingly gives up their life for the life of their child.

A true parent sacrifices, endures hurt, pain, and shame to do whatever is best for their child.

I know there are a lot of true parents in the world. We have endured a lot and sacrificed greatly for our children.

I was 15 years old when I found out I was pregnant.

I was so afraid. I was afraid of what my parents would say, afraid of what my church members would think, and afraid of what a baby meant for my life overall.

I was so involved and had so much going for me. I was a cheerleader, played in the band, an active member of student council, and so much more.

Everyone knew me. They also knew and loved the guy I was dating.

Initially, when I told him I was pregnant, he appeared supportive. He went to the doctor with me to make sure the test was positive. He held my hand and did his best to assure me that everything was going to be okay.

However, once he found out how far along I was and that abortion was possible, he immediately started to remind me of the life we had and the future we planned.

He talked about our plans to go to college and how a baby was going to ruin all of it.

At first I thought he was right, and I went home with a heavy heart thinking about what was best.

As time went on, the gravity of aborting my child tugged at me. I started to think about the precious life inside me, and I knew abortion was not an option.

I went to my boyfriend and explained to him I could not have an abortion. He did not understand, and he thought I was being unreasonable. He said I was only thinking of myself and not of his future. He decided to walk away and not look back.

I was left alone to face the aftermath of my choice.

I had to tell my parents, my coach, my teachers, my counselor, and my Pastor. In that moment, I became a tough girl.

I chose to allow my child to live, not knowing the type of future we would have long-term.

As a young, 10th grade student, I knew nothing about being a mom. However, I knew I wanted my child to live no matter the cost.

There were some lonely times during the next six months.

Friends walked away. My parents and grandparents looked at me with tears of disappointment and concern in their eyes.

A teacher had to come to my house, so I could continue with my education.

I faced lonely, tired, and restless days, but I knew I made the right choice. I wanted my child to live, and two weeks before my 16th birthday I gave birth to a 7 pound 2 ounces baby girl.

I will never forget the moment I looked at her precious little face.

I knew my choice was not only the right choice, but it was also the best choice.

There were so many things I had to let go. There were so

many changes I had to make, but I was ready.

I was ready to fight for our future; I was ready to show the world I would win this round.

I knew I was going to prove I would not be defeated. My choice made me stronger and more determined than ever.

I could not look back. I could only focus on what God had for us.

Yes, I disobeyed God's word by having sex before marriage. However, I knew when I asked for forgiveness, God forgave me. I knew He was with me, and with His help we were going to make it.

God's love is so sovereign. He is just and faithful.

I made one bad choice, but I was so thankful He spoke to my heart, helping me not to make two mistakes.

My daughter is a wonderful woman. She is educated, a wife, a mother, a sister, a teacher, a coach, an entrepreneur, an author, and so much more to so many. She was not a statistic like most said she would become due to my choice.

Imagine if I had made the choice to not allow her to live. The world, my world, would be so different.

Every day we are faced with so many choices. A lot of times I am not sure if we are aware that choosing life is always the best choice.

Deuteronomy 30:19 states, "This day I call the heavens and the earth as witnesses against you, that I have set before you life and death, blessings and curses. Now choose life so that you and your children may live."

I chose to allow the little baby inside me to live. Maybe your life choice is different, but whatever the choice, if we choose life we always win.

I chose life, and I won the round.

The enemy thought this round was going to take me out. He thought I would run over in a corner and give up. He thought I would take off my gloves and resend to the punches he threw.

Little did he know; his blows would not knock me out.

At 15 years old, I became a tough a girl.

Ropes Course

Take an opportunity to reflect and respond to the questions and statements below.

What type of life choices have you made?

How has your life been impacted by your choices and decisions?

ROUND 4
Disability

*I*n John chapter 9, Jesus' disciples asked, "Jesus who sinned? Was it the blind man or his mother and father?"

Jesus answered, "Neither this man nor his parents sinned. This happened so that the works of God might be displayed in him."

There are so many people who think like the disciples, and there are so many parents of disabled children who wonder if they failed God in their faithfulness or obedience to Him.

I have not always lived for God or been the person He desired. Still, today, I am striving to become more like Him.

My two oldest sons have Fragile-X syndrome. We had no idea at birth that either of them had this condition. It was not until they started to grow that I realized there were some developmental delays.

My oldest son was born weighing 8 pounds 2 ounces. At 18 months, he was not talking. He would attempt to make words, but we could not understand him.

I took him to so many doctors and specialists. I wanted to find out what was happening with my baby.

The doctors told me he had fluid on his ear drums, and it was keeping him from hearing properly, which in turn was keeping him from talking. We immediately agreed to have surgery to remove the fluid. I just knew after the surgery he would be better.

I worked with him to help him catch up on the things he struggled to learn. A year later he was forming words, but it appeared he had a difficult time comprehending instruction.

I did not understand. I worked with him intensely, and I made sure everything was corrected from the surgery. However, we were still struggling to help him reach the appropriate level.

The doctors could not tell me anything. We tried every test possible to figure out what was wrong.

Amid everything happening, I found myself pregnant with another son.

My second son was born almost 8 weeks early; he weighed 5 pounds.

Although he was born early, the doctors did not expect any

delays, as he was fully developed.

Still trying to get the information I needed to help my oldest son, I started to realize my new little bundle was having problems too. I did not understand. I was so confused by their conditions.

Questions and thoughts raced through my mind.

What am I doing wrong?

Am I not eating appropriately during pregnancy?

Am I not getting enough prenatal care or exercising properly?

I was so confused. I could not believe the same situation was happening again.

I was older than I was when I delivered my first child, surely, I knew how to take better care of myself.

What is going on?

The doctors could not give me any answers. We had test after test completed for both boys, but there were still no answers.

My oldest son started four-year-old kindergarten. I believed things would change, as the teacher was trained to lead instruction. Therefore, I believed he would get the hands-on experience he needed to excel.

Instead, the teacher called me after a few months and shared she believed he needed more help than she could provide.

Immediately, I placed him in therapy to help with the development of his motor skills and the like.

Again, I thought more one-on-one support would help increase his proficiency. However, by the end of the school year he had made very little progress.

My second son was now three, and I learned about a program he could begin.

I thought if we got a head start with his education, things would be different, better.

I was right. My second son made great strides. He was still not reaching all his milestones, but he was progressing.

I had a third son; he weighed 6 pounds 7 ounces. I thought I needed to prepare myself for what could be, but as he started to grow, I could tell there were no delays. He progressed very quickly, and as the years went on, I watched him excel in so many areas.

Many years passed. We made it through elementary school, but my two oldest sons still struggled academically.

Finally, we came across a doctor who encouraged me to have genetic testing.

From those tests, I found out my sons had Fragile-X syndrome, a genetic disorder.

I learned it was a gene disorder I carried, and I could only pass it on to my sons, which is why my daughter did not have any delays.

However, based on the results of the test, I could not understand why my youngest son displayed no signs of delayed learning or mastery of skills. Even the doctors had no explanation as to why my youngest son showed no signs of the syndrome.

Doctors were shocked and amazed by my boys. With my oldest sons, they could not believe they were so much more developed than others who suffered with the same condition. With my youngest son, they could not believe he had no signs of the syndrome whatsoever.

Doctors told me all three of my sons should be disabled, and all three of them should be developmentally delayed. He did not understand how my oldest two were so high functioning, nor did he understand why my baby boy did not have the disorder at all.

I too was shocked, but then I remembered the day in my mother's kitchen when I asked God for help. I knew my boys did not suffer severely, and not at all in the youngest one's case, because God turned the situation around.

My two older boys are still delayed today, but it is amazing to see what God has done in their lives.

My middle son became a gymnast. He traveled the world with Special Olympics displaying his talents, and he has won several gold medals.

Both my oldest and middle son graduated from high school, they work every day, earn their own money, and they live on their own with little assistance.

My youngest son attends college, and he is employed. I know God has greatness ahead of him because he loves and protects his brothers. He even works as a caregiver for disabled adults.

My daughter too is sensitive to the needs of children who suffer with disabilities, and in her profession, does her best to get them the help they need to succeed.

I have even had a young man tell me he became a Special Education teacher because of my children.

They have taught us so much, as a family, but they have also taught the community we live in that being disabled does not mean one is unable to succeed.

My boys grew our family; they changed the way we looked at life, people, and their abilities.

Going through these rounds with my sons was not just a tough girl moment, it was a tough girl journey.

The situation was so overwhelming sometimes. I really thought it was going to be a knockout!

I fought with doctors, teachers, therapists, and society when they did not understand my boys.

I have watched my other two children cry because they wanted to fight people because of the way they treated their brothers.

There were many nights I went to bed tired and crying simply because I did not understand what was going on with them or what I did wrong.

I now know their condition has nothing to with me. God was not punishing me or my family; He was making us better.

He was mending the hurt and disappointment we suffered from people who walked out on us, and folks who said we would never make it.

He was mending the pain of knowing people counted us out because they believed the 15 year old pregnant girl, with three more children by 24 years of age, would become a statistic.

What was meant to disable us gave us the ability to understand people, to love people for who they are, and how they are. It showed us how to stick together and look to God, especially when we cannot find the answer.

God healed us, just like He did the blind man. He made us

whole, and He opened our eyes to a wonderful world of potential—being able to see potential in all.

We all have a disability, but just as Jesus healed the blind man, He will heal you if you open your heart to accepting Him.

I cannot think of one thing God touches that does not become better.

He is making you better!

Ropes Course

Take an opportunity to reflect and respond to the questions and statements below.

What situation attempted to disable you?

How have those situations caused you to question God?

How has God allowed you to see that He is getting the glory out of your situation?

ROUND 5
The Sacrifice

Mary, the mother of Jesus sat at the foot of the cross and watched her child endure beatings, be despised, lied on, and ridiculed.

I can only imagine how she must have felt watching her child, who had done no wrong, experience such a painful and tragic death.

Mary, the biblical tough girl, reminds me of my grandmother.

My grandmother was a strong woman. She worked hard, and she loved God.

I remember being a little girl, watching my grandmother go to work every day. Some days she even walked to work, only to return home to cook a meal, make certain I completed my homework, showered, and combed my hair.

She did these things for me because my mom and dad worked second shift. That routine went on for many years. For the most part, I spent time with my parents on the weekend because of their work schedules.

One day, I recall coming home from school and my mom was in my grandmother's bed.

I went into the bedroom to ask if she was okay, but she just laid there with tears in her eyes and a blank look on her face.

I was just a little girl, only 8 years old. However, I knew something terrible had happened. The woman there in the bed was not my mom—the happy woman who laughed and played with me even when she was tired.

I immediately went to my grandmother and asked what was wrong. My grandmother told me to let my mom rest.

My grandmother went on with our daily routine. Several days passed and mom's mood had not changed. She would get out of bed, shower, and go right back to bed. A few times she came into the living room and sat in a chair, but she did not say anything.

Again, I asked my grandmother what was wrong. I was very confused why my mom would not talk to me.

My grandmother then explained that my parents were getting

a divorce.

She explained that my mother was depressed, and she told me what depression actually meant. She assured me that my mom would be fine, and she was encouraging her to see a doctor.

I watched my grandmother take my mom's food into her room and try and talk to her, but my mom would not respond.

All of the thoughts going on in her mind were holding her hostage.

I did not know what to think, or how to help.

My grandmother did her best to hold things together, and make everything appear normal. However, I could see in her face that her heart was breaking.

This was her only daughter, and she had already attempted to take her life twice. My grandmother was afraid and broken.

I remember my grandmother calling several preachers to come to our house to pray, and there were many nights I heard her praying, crying, and calling out to God to deliver her child from this terrible illness.

It appeared that my mother had died on the inside, and there was nothing that would bring her back to us. We watched her suffer through this terrible situation for years before she found the strength to face the world again. However, as we waited, there were many tears shed. There were also a lot days that

I did not understand what she was going through, or how to help.

A lot of people talked about my mom. They called her crazy. Some even said she was faking because she did not want to go back to work or take care of me. My grandmother continued to defend her, and she took care of her until she was delivered from the state of depression that had such a terrible grip.

I do not believe my grandmother really understood what was going on with my mother, but she understood that my mom was her child and she was going to support her. She was determined to be with my mom no matter what people said or thought.

She was not leaving her side. She believed God's word, and she knew His healing would be manifested in my mom's life. It took years, but God delivered my mother and He set her free from the bondage in her mind.

Today, she is saved and lives for God. My mother realized depression was from the enemy, and she knew she had too much to live for to just give up and allow the enemy to win.

She gained her strength from Psalm 27:
> *1 The Lord is my light and my salvation—whom shall I fear? The Lord is the stronghold of my life—of whom shall I be afraid?*
>
> *2 When the wicked advance against me to devour me, it is my enemies and my foes who will stumble and fall.*

*3 Though an army besiege me, my heart will not fear;
though war break out against me, even then I will be
confident.*

*4 One thing I ask from the Lord, this only do I seek: that I
may dwell in the house of the Lord all the days of my
life, to gaze on the beauty of the Lord and to seek him in
his temple.*

*5 For in the day of trouble he will keep me safe in his
dwelling; he will hide me in the shelter of his sacred tent
and set me high upon a rock.*

*6 Then my head will be exalted above the enemies who
surround me; at his sacred tent I will sacrifice with
shouts of joy; I will sing and make music to the Lord.*

*7 Hear my voice when I call, Lord; be merciful to me and
answer me.*

*8 My heart says of you, "Seek his face!" Your face, Lord, I
will seek.*

*9 Do not hide your face from me, do not turn your servant
away in anger; you have been my helper. Do not reject
me or forsake me, God my Savior.*

*10 Though my father and mother forsake me, the Lord will
receive me.*

11 Teach me your way, Lord; lead me in a straight path because of my oppressors.

12 Do not turn me over to the desire of my foes, for false witnesses rise up against me, spouting malicious accusations.

13 I remain confident of this: I will see the goodness of the Lord in the land of the living.

14 Wait for the Lord; be strong and take heart and wait for the Lord.

God's word healed and delivered my mother!

Have you ever witnessed someone you love suffer through a situation?

Have you wished you could change the situation for them, but there is nothing you can do other than remain present, no matter the outcome?

Depression is a horrible disease that we do not always understand.

It is an enemy that kills your hope, steals your joy, and destroys your relationships.

In this round, my grandmother, mother, and I were all fighting. At the time, I was a little girl, and there was no way I could have fought that round alone.

That round could have knocked me out in such a way I may have never fought again.

However, I had a great coach! My grandmother's example showed me how to stay in the ring.

By living through pain and not walking away, I watched her stay in the ring and continue the fight.

Watching my grandmother, I learned life may knock you down, the blows may be hard and constant, but you do not stay there. You keep getting up, and you fight back.

We never lose if we fight back.

Sometimes we may have to stay in the ring longer than we desire, but we have to stay in and keep fighting.

My mom wanted to give up, but she remained in the ring. She continued to fight, and now she is whole and living a life of peace and joy.

Just think, she wanted to throw in the towel and die in her sickness. However, my grandmother saw she was worn and decided to fight for her until she regained her strength. I can imagine it was not easy seeing her child in that state, but she remained tough.

Just as Mary watched her son carry the cross up the hill, bleeding, beaten, and in pain, she knew God would deliver Him because of His assignment to save the world. Yet, knowing God would deliver Him did not ease her pain in the moment. However, she remained tough.

Watching those we love go through challenges is not always easy, but it is worth it. To have your loved one receive eternal life because you fought for them when they were too weak, too hurt, or too broken to fight on their own brings so much peace and joy to your life.

We are our sister's keepers. Therefore, we will make sacrifices to fight for them and with them to defeat the enemy. While sacrifices can be difficult, our faith and trust in God is developed and strengthened—we become tougher.

Ropes Course

Take an opportunity to reflect and respond to the questions and statements below.

How can you find the strength to fight for yourself?

What does fighting for yourself look like?

How can you find the strength to fight for someone else?

What would getting into the ring to fight for someone else look like for you?

ROUND 6
Twelve Years

There was a woman in the bible who suffered for 12 years with an illness; she spent all her money going to doctors to understand her symptoms and find resolve.

There in her town, she heard about Jesus, a man known for healing those who were sick and raising the dead.

Immediately, the woman wanted to meet Jesus. She made her way to the nearby town where Jesus was visiting. When she arrived, the crowd was so thick she could not reach Him. She pressed her way through the crowd. I believe there were so many people she likely fell to her knees, crawling to get to Him.

Once she reached Jesus, she touched the hem of His garment. She was healed instantly.

It is amazing how one touch from Jesus can change our lives. I was twelve years old when I accepted Jesus as my Savior. It was a Wednesday night during Vacation Bible School.

I do not recall the lesson from that evening. However, I remember feeling like there was someone greater than myself, who I needed to embrace.

That night, I was introduced to Jesus.

Excited about my newly found faith, I became more involved in church. I was always a part of church, my grandmother made sure of that, but I became more active in the youth group, and I started singing in the choir.

Things were wonderful.

For almost two years I was living out my salvation, and it was amazing. Then I entered high school; my whole life changed.

There were so many distractions. I got involved in so many activities, met so many new people, and I was being invited to parties and ball games. It was great!

However, as I became a part of my new world, I became more and more distant from my friend Jesus.

Before long, I found myself hardly going to church and barely being involved. I was hanging out, I started drinking, and partying.

Sadly, I made my new friends more important than my Savior—the one who helped me through so many trying times in my life.

This new way seemed exciting and fresh, and it felt like something I had never experienced.

I was going places, and I was being exposed to things and situations I did not know people were engaged in at all.

My grandmother had me so sheltered, and she always did her best to live a Godly life before me.

I lived that life for years. Hanging out with the wrong people, in the wrong places, allowing myself to get deeper and deeper into a space of hurt, pain, and sickness.

Twelve years later, at 24 years old, standing in my mother's kitchen, I started to have an anxiety attack. I could not breathe. I felt like I was dying.

My life was replaying in my head, all the choices I made—good and bad.

I thought about the life I dreamed of having at 12 years old, and how my current life and lifestyle did not line up to the path I wanted for myself. I did not have the life I dreamed about all those years ago.

At that point, I was the mother of four, working a minimum wage job, living with my mother. Alone and afraid of what the future meant for me and my children, I could not breathe, and I did not know how things were going to end for us.

As I stood there crying, gasping for air, I heard a still small voice say, "Go back to your first love."

My first real love was Jesus, as He was the one I met that Wednesday night during Vacation Bible School.

I knew He was greater than me, and I knew He was sent so that I could live a peaceful life, even during struggle. I called on Him, and I promised Him that if He showed me the way out of the mess I made, I would live for Him.

That day He touched me, and He allowed me to touch Him.

Piece by piece, He started showing me the way.

He reminded me that if He was before me, nothing and no one could be against me.

He reminded me of His blood, and He reaffirmed that I was an overcomer. In His presence, I knew I was not condemned because of the choices I made. I was redeemed because of His shed blood.

He started showing me my gifts and talents, and He reminded me that I could do all things through Him.

It was amazing how I started to see myself. I no longer saw my circumstances; I saw where I was going and became content with the blessings of the Lord.

I knew I could not become complacent because God was showing me so much more for my life. I gained clarity and direction from His word, and it changed my life and guided me into a life of meaning, joy, peace, and stability.

I found Jesus at 12 years old, but suffered for 12 years because I did not stay the course with Him. I learned quickly He was and is my strength in weakness, and I am only tough with Him (2 Corinthians 12:9).

No matter how long you have been in a place of uncertainty or struggle, just like the woman with the sickness for twelve long years, press your way to touch the hem of His garment.

A fresh start, a new beginning, is available for us all. Reach out and touch Him today!

Ropes Course

Take an opportunity to reflect and respond to the questions and statements below.

Will you allow Jesus to touch you, and will you reach out and touch Him?

What will His touch mean for your life?

ROUND 7
My Naomi

Naomi was Elimelek's wife. They had two sons, Mahlon and Kilion.

Elimelek died, leaving Naomi with their sons.

Mahlon and Kilion married two Moabite women, Orpah and Ruth (Ruth 1:3-5).

After ten years of living with their mother, Mahlon and Kilion died, and Naomi decided to return home to Bethlehem.

Because her sons were dead, she encouraged her daughters-in-law to return to their homeland. Oprah agreed to return, and she kissed Naomi goodbye. Ruth, however, decided to follow Naomi, and she was blessed due to her decision.

I met a wonderful woman when I was young. Although I was

dating her son, she and I developed a close relationship.

She was full of wisdom, but more than anything, she was full of love.

We had only known each other for a few months when we started spending a lot of time together. She taught me how to become a wife, and a mother, who cared for her family.

We spoke, at length, about life, my future, and my hopes and dreams.

She talked to me about setting goals for myself and furthering my education.

We talked about cooking and cleaning. She even taught me how to decorate my home for the holidays.

However, above everything else, we talked about God, and how having a relationship with Him was more important than anything in the world.

She was awesome, and I loved her so much.

Her son and I eventually broke up, but it did not change our relationship. I think we became even closer.

One day she told me she had been diagnosed with cancer; I will never forget that day.

I was so worried. I cried forever because I was afraid.

However, she was strong, and she told me not to worry. She said she was going to have surgery and take treatments. She told me knew God was going to spare her life. We started praying and asking God for complete healing.

The surgery went well, but the chemotherapy and radiation made her ill. I remember getting off work going to check on her to see if there was anything I could do to help.

She was always so gracious. She would smile, and she wanted me to sit and talk with her and her husband.

After she completed her round of treatment, the doctor stated the cancer was gone, and my friend started to feel better. She even gained enough strength to return to work.

However, after about a year, the cancer returned and the doctor said she only had a few months to live. She assured me again God was going to heal her. I was in complete agreement because I knew God had done it before, and we believed He would do it again.

As the days went by, she grew weaker, and the doctors did not want to operate.

I would visit with her for hours at a time, sitting by her bedside. Sometimes I would not even talk. I simply held her hand, thinking of all our conversations, and all the things she expected of me, and desired for me to achieve.

I could not believe the woman I had only known for such a

short period of time taught me so much. I wondered how I would live without her, if God called her home.

What would my children and I do without her?

She was such a great part of my life.

She loved on us and gave us so much of herself. I could not imagine my world without her in it.

I will never forget the day she told me she had received her healing. I was so happy and excited.

I thought it was wonderful, and I knew it would just be a matter of time before she started to regain her strength. I started to talk about all the things she and I would do with the kids.

She softly said, "No LaVerne. I will be healed, but I won't be here with you. God says it is time to come home. There, I will be made whole."

My heart was broken. I cried so much that day because she had become my best friend.

I was losing my best friend, and my prayer partner.

Again, I was left unclear. I did not understand how cancer could take her down. She was only in her forties, and I needed her.

I needed her to continue to share her wisdom and her love.

Indeed, it was a tough moment. Then, I realized why I chose to stay with her despite her son and I splitting. She was my Naomi.

My friend died March of 1994. However, because I chose to remain her friend, I have been blessed by the love we shared.

I could have disconnected from her, but like Ruth, I saw something in her that allowed me to see myself and understand the way I viewed motherhood and having a family was not what God ordained. So, I decided to follow her.

The life she lived was God's way for family, and I needed her to help me with the process.

Like Naomi helped Ruth find her true love, she helped me find my true purpose—being a good mother and one day a good wife.

The day she died was a very hard day for me; I do not know if anyone knew how hard it was.

However, I know if I had not made the choice to remain her friend, even while being uncomfortable, I would not have learned what I needed to grow as a tough girl.

Sometimes, being uncomfortable is required to become all God wants us to become.

The choice I made to stay close to my Naomi and learn from her did not always feel so good, but I know it was the plan God set forth.

I am so grateful I listened.

Ropes Course

Take an opportunity to reflect and respond to the questions and statements below.

Which of your choices have made you uncomfortable?

Have you struggled, or are you struggling with leaving the familiar for the unfamiliar?

What have you learned from your choice to embrace the unfamiliar?

ROUND 8
Sarah

To my understanding, Sarah was a beautiful woman. She was Abraham's wife, and they received a promise from God. God promised Sarah and Abraham they would have a child.

However, Sarah and Abraham were older when God made the promise. At the time, Sarah was about 75 years old.

Sarah loved God, which was clear through her devotion to her husband. However, when God told Sarah she would bear a child in her old age, she thought it was funny, and after many years of waiting she started to doubt God's promise.

Sarah then took it upon herself to help God, so she had her husband lay with their handmaid, Hagar.

The request caused Abraham and Sarah so much grief because

it was not the plan God had for their lives.

I have always been the kind of woman who likes to help those in need.

One day, someone I knew very well called me in need of a place to live.

It was a young, married woman with children. She had recently found out her husband cheated on her, and she needed a different place to live.

At the time, my husband and I owned some rental property, so I spoke with him about allowing her and her children to live there. He agreed, and the family moved in the home.

Everything appeared to be going well. We were helping her have a secure and safe place to live, and was helping us by paying her rent timely.

The arrangement seemed to benefit everyone. Looking back, I realize our plan was to help our family and the other family, but I did not seek God's guidance before making an agreement with this woman.

I assumed because she had a need, and we had a need, it was God's way of helping us meet our obligation with multiple properties.

Little did I know; this agreement would cause me to become a divorced woman.

Once the young lady and her children settled in, I noticed my ex-husband would go to the house to help her keep the grass cut and take her trash to the landfill.

I explained to him that although we knew her, she was still a tenant, and she needed to fulfil those obligations on her own. He said he was only trying to help her because she was accustomed to having someone help her with those things.

I calmed down about the matter, and asked him to show her what she needed to do to maintain the upkeep of the home.

I did not want to become too critical, because I too had been a single parent at one time, and having someone help with those types of things would have been a blessing to me.

After a few short months, she started to fall behind in her rent.

She started calling my ex-husband if her car would not start, which had nothing to do with her rental agreement. When I questioned him again, he assured me he was only trying to help her because she was alone with the children and needed our help.

However, when she could not afford to pay her rent one month, I realized something was wrong.

She told me she explained everything to my husband, and he had assured her we would give her time. However, when I spoke with him about the matter, he acted as if he had no knowledge of their conversation to extend the rent.

The rent continued to fall further and further behind; I had no choice but to file eviction papers.

I then found out, he had been promising her if she would be his mistress he would make sure she lived in the home rent free.

I was devastated! I could not believe he would do that to me, and I was shocked that she too had kept it a secret because I knew her extremely well.

The betrayal cut deep, and it broke my heart.

My husband, the man I had been with for 16 years cheated on me.

He had done things in the past, things that hurt, things I questioned, but that part of our marriage I thought was sacred.

I was faithful to him. I never allowed another man to enter our bed of marriage.

I was flooded with so many emotions. I was angry, hurt, and disappointed. I felt betrayed, and I began to question everything about our marriage. I realized I could not live this way, and our lives would not be the same.

I would cry every time he touched me, because I thought about him touching someone else the way he touched me.

He spoke the same, sweet words to some other woman. I

thought his words were just for me.

I wondered if there were other women. I did not know what to think.

I decided we could no longer remain as husband and wife. It was too hard, and it hurt too much.

After the divorce was final, I sat and thought about everything that took place.

I recalled the story of Abraham and Sarah, and although I did not give this woman my husband, I did allow this situation into our space because I did not seek God.

I did not pray and ask for guidance, I did not even ask God to bless the decision I made once I had made the choice.

Have you ever made a decision you later regretted?

A decision you genuinely thought was God answering a prayer because everything seemed so clear and logical.

I am sure that is what Sarah thought when she gave Abraham their handmaid, and while her decision brought forth Ishmael, he was not the promise.

Sometimes we are so anxious for a solution or an answer to a problem, we forfeit the promise of God.

Lean not to your own understanding, but in all your ways

acknowledge Him, and allow God to direct your path (Proverbs 3:6).

Once you have prayed, and even if you feel like you did not hear God, ask Him to bless your decision. You will have peace knowing you called on Him.

I did not get knocked out in this round, but I felt every blow. There were times I was knocked down, but I was determined to continue to get up and fight.

I am still fighting. I am fighting to forget those things that are behind me, and I am pressing towards the mark of the higher calling in Christ Jesus (Philippians 3:13-14).

I am fighting to remain confident in who God made me, and I am fighting to remind myself that I am victorious even when I get knocked down.

Some may say I lost, but we never lose until we stop fighting.

Every round, with God on our side, we become tougher.

Ropes Course

Take an opportunity to reflect and respond to the questions and statements below.

Which rounds of life have left you feeling every blow?

How are you fighting to ensure you reach God's promise?

ROUND 9
The Final Round

In Isaiah 43:2, God tells us that He will be with us as we go through the water and through the fire.

Meaning, in this life, there will be trials and tribulations we cannot avoid—even as Christians.

I have been through many tests and trials, and I believe you have too.

There have been times I faced loneliness, depression, grief, hurt, disappointment, and persecution.

I have faced hardship, loss, and financial burdens, despite me trying to do my best to love and serve God.

Situations arise.

However, as a Christian, I have learned that everything I have faced and everything I will face, is designed to make me a better me—stronger.

Those seemingly low valleys are in place to grow me up because fires and floods build Godly character.

Godly character, helps us bear good fruit–love, joy, peace, longsuffering, kindness, goodness, gentleness, faithfulness, and self-control.

If we never go through anything, we will lack the evidence of the fruit that lives in us because there will be nothing to help us produce that which is planted.

Our troubles and trails help serve as examples for those around us, and they help us to become more like Jesus. In Isaiah chapter 43 God is speaking to Israel, but His message applies to all of His children.

God delivered Israel in the past when they crossed the Red Sea and the Jordan River. I believe many times we cross dangerous areas throughout our lives, without even knowing it.

I also believe God parts the waters, straightens the crooked places, and sometimes defeats the enemy without our knowledge.

Indeed, He is an AWESOME GOD!

When we pass through the water, we will get wet. We may be wet with worries, wet with frustration, and sometimes we may get caught in a rain shower of problems where we are soaked with the crisis and cares of life.

Rest assured, it will not take you out!

It might slow you down, and it might alter your route. However, God has promised to remain with you. He will even dry you off, and give you a change of clothes.

When you pass through the fire, you will feel the heat, the flames may singe you, and the heat may intimidate you, but God will remain despite the intensity!

In spite of the furnace, He is God.

In spite of the flames of discouragement and disappointment surrounding you, He is God.

He will keep you from being consumed.

You can rest assured that He is present, even in the tough places of life.

God is our protector.

His protection is our gift of reassurance!

There is glory in His record.

Sometimes I have to review His record; His record gives me help for my present and hope for my future.

The record of God becomes the very thing that helps me hold out and to hang on.

Sometimes the rope of life gets short and slippery, but then I remember His record.

David said in Psalm 40, "I waited and I waited, and I kept on waiting upon the Lord, and He heard my cry. He lifted me out of a slimy pit, out of the mud of life. He set my feet on a rock and gave me a place to stand. He put a new song in my mouth."

He went on to say in Psalm 46, "God is our refuge and strength, an ever-present help in trouble."

In Psalm 23, he declared, "The Lord is my Shepherd, and I shall not want."

He asked in Psalm 27, "The Lord is my light and my salvation, whom shall I fear? The Lord is the strength of my life of whom shall I be afraid?"

Therefore, like David, if an army besieged me, my heart will not fear.

Look at the record of your life!

God has delivered other individuals, as proven in scripture, and He will surely deliver us.

Through every situation, tragedy, and triumph we face, there is a similar, if not the same situation in God's word.

Those stories were recorded so you and I could gain clarity and understand how to maneuver through problems we would face.

We are tough by design! Therefore, we have what it takes to fight through every situation and come out of the ring victorious.

We are never knocked out, and with Jesus we are more than conquerors in every situation because His death, burial, and resurrection insures, assures, and ensures our victory.

Jesus faced everything we could ever face. He walked the earth understanding and experiencing how things have the ability to hurt us, how dreams can be delayed, and how we can become tempted.

However, knowing He won every battle, and gave His life for ours, should give us confidence in knowing we are a part of a winning dynasty.

No matter how long you have to stay in the ring, no matter how many times you have to pull yourself up by the ropes before the bell rings, get back up because you are a winner!

This fight is not given to the swift or the strong, but it is given to those of us who are tough enough to endure to the end.

Through it all, keep fighting TOUGH GIRL!

The fight is fixed; you WIN!

About the Author

Minister LaVerne Richardson is a native of Spartanburg, South Carolina. She is the daughter of Mrs. Janie Richardson and the late Leonard Richardson.

God has blessed her with four children, Jossalyn, Brandon, Rashad, and Marquis. She also has a son-in-law Darryl, and she is the proud grandmother of Mr. Christopher Luke Wilson.

Minister LaVerne has been an employee of the Federal Government of the United States for over 20 years.

She is a member and Associate Minister of the First Baptist Church of Fairforest, where Pastor W.I. and Co-Pastor Danita Jenkins lead.

Under their leadership, Minister LaVerne was called and

licensed to preach in 2012.

Since, she has been preaching and teaching the Word of God.

She loves her church family, works with the Teen Choir, Women's Ministry, and Youth Ministry. She is also an assistant Sunday school teacher.

Minster Laverne is also the Founder of Walk In the Light Family Ministry, a non-profit organization established in 2007.

She is currently establishing a new non-profit organization, Tough Girls, to empower and encourage women everywhere.

She is establishing Tough Girls to support other organizations that work to equip and encourage young men and women, like Accelerating Men and Jossalyn's Journey.

Ultimately, Minister LaVerne's passion is to see people reach their expected end.

Adding to her list of accomplishments, she has authored *Tough Girls,* a book designed to inspire parents and audiences everywhere. She wants to help parents and individuals understand that the journey of parenthood and life may not be easy, but they can succeed.

Her main focus is serving the Lord, something she counts as an honor and a privilege.

Of Minister LaVerne's many roles, she feels her greatest title is Mom, but states, "Nana feels really good too."

One of her favorite scriptures is Isaiah 53:5, "For he was wounded for our transgressions, bruised for our iniquities and the chastisement of our peace was upon him and by his stripes, we are healed."

Minister LaVerne is excited about God's plans, and she is thankful to partner with Him to fulfill her purpose.

Notes

www.ingramcontent.com/pod-product-compliance
Lightning Source LLC
Chambersburg PA
CBHW070547300426
44113CB00011B/1812